IMPRESSIONS
of the Heart

by Lacey Whittaker

Edited by Lil Barcaski and Linda Hinkle

Published by: GWN Publishing

www.GWNPublishing.com

Cover Design: Kristina Conatser Captured by KC Design

ISBN: 979-8-9863922-8-8

Dedication

To all those who long for a heart like Jesus.

Introduction

Search me and know my heart, Lord. I yearn for a heart like Yours Jesus. My heart cries out, do You hear me, Lord?

What tugs on your heart? The Lord gave us a heart for all people. He gave us a heart to love them and pray for them. Does your heart love the unlovable? In this book, you will find many prayers that relate to the battles of the heart that we all face. You will find love in His sweet name. Your heart will feel grace.

WHAT TUGS ON YOUR HEART? Is it the lady at the stop sign? The widow in the store? Maybe the child you see that feels nothing anymore? What about those ones forgotten in their homes, or the sick ones that don't have a loved one cheering them along? What tugs on your heart? The Lord gave us a heart for these people, these things. He gave us a heart to love them and pray.

I WANT TO BE WISE. I want you to rejoice. I want you to say, look at how she carries her voice. How she speaks truth, shows kindness, and repents. To be wise is to choose to rejoice in Him.

"My child, if your heart is wise,
my own heart will rejoice!"

PROVERBS 23:15 NLT

Are you impressed with His will or your way? Are you fighting against Him and choosing to stay? Do you portray in evil wicked things? Bow down and choose His wisdom today.

The heart of a bully is to harass, intimidate, threaten, torment, and throw shade. The heart of a bully. Where does this heart come from? Where did this heart go so wrong? It's easy to place the blame. It's easy to go after, and battle, and fight when your daughter is on the receiving end of the bullies' attacks. In my flesh, I want to fight to take the bully down. I want to repay evil with evil. That's what it is. It's evil. They have learned this; they have felt this. The bully is the hurting one. So, Lord, when the bully comes against my baby girl, help me remember there is so much more to deal. For them to know Your loving will. Help me pray for them, forgive them, and show You. Help me Jesus. Help me ring true. With my whole heart I want to honor You.

"Let nothing be done through selfish ambition or conceit,
but in lowliness of mind let each esteem others better
than himself."

PHILIPPIANS 2:3 NKJV

ARE YOU HUMBLE OR FULL OF PRIDE? Where does your heart lie? Are you fake, jealous, and ruled by selfishness? Are you humble and low, thinking highly of others instead of your way? Choose today to stay humble and true. Choose today to honor the Jesus that died for you.

The punches kept coming, one after another, and another. We found ourselves sitting in that hospital room with our 10-year-old baby girl. Her face was sunken in, she was gray, scared, dehydrated, and skinny as a rail. So helpless laying there. As the doctor walked in with the news, we wondered if he was an angel. So gentle, here to soften the blow of the news that was going to change our lives as we knew it. Then he said, "your daughter has Type 1 Diabetes." We just sat there and cried. If I could take this from her I would've. I cried out to God, please take this from her and give to me. We watched the countless finger pricks and the abundance of shots. We soon realized this was going to be our new normal. As we took our girl home, the worry, panic, and anxiety set in. Would she make it through the night? How was she going to be able to go to school? What if? What if something happens? What if? I couldn't control this. I couldn't control this if I tried. What if it consumed me all my days and nights? As I look back, only the Lord could've got us through those four months of hell. My mind still wanders from time to time, and I freak out. When the panic comes on, I remember to pray and take a deep breath of trust and faith. My daughter is His. He has her. He will protect her. He loves her. He knows. I trust her with Him; this I know.

GUILT IS HARD. Mom guilt is harder. Why did I stay? Why did I let him treat my kids that way? Why, oh why, only He knows. Why couldn't I let go? Why, oh why, did it take me so long? Why did it take me to knocking down the door to see my child trying to commit suicide? Why, oh why, I ask these things? Why, oh why? Lord, help me find a way. Thank You for saving her that day.

I'M A FIXER. I want to fix everything and everyone. I want to fix it all. I want to fix. How can I truly fix or help anyone if I don't work on myself first? How, how, how? Why, oh why, oh why is this so hard? Why is it so hard to forgive and go through all the dark days? Why is it so hard to see there is a new way? Help me, Lord. Help me. I have seen Your grace. I have seen. Help me, Lord. Help me today.

"For with the heart one believes unto righteousness, and with the mouth confession is made unto salvation."

ROMANS 10:10 NKJV

I believe You are who You say You are. I believe we are made whole in the crucifixion of Jesus Christ. I believe You died and rose again. I believe one day we will be in heaven with You.

The past triggers me and I become angry. I become so angry with all the abuse I endured. All the control, the guilt, the lost time. I thought he would change, so I stayed, and I buried it deep in my gut. So helpless and with nowhere to turn, I buried it. I held on. I held on so tight thinking one day things would be right. It only left me angry with unforgiveness all these years. Lord, please show me how to forgive and heal.

I feel like some family members can cut us the deepest and hurt our hearts more than outsiders. Why our family? The ones that are supposed to love us no matter what.

FAMILY. The ones that are supposed to be by our sides no matter what. The ones that are supposed to love unconditionally. The ones that are supposed to laugh with you. The ones that are supposed to cry with you. The ones that are supposed to be your biggest supporters. The ones that are supposed to choose you over anyone else. The ones that are supposed to pick you up when you are down. Lord, help our family love us unconditionally. Lord, help our family laugh and cry with us. Lord, help our family be our biggest supporters. Lord, help our family put family first. Lord, heal our hearts that family has broken. Lord, help our family.

Why did you have to leave? In a sudden moment. I didn't know that was going to be the last time I heard, "I love her with all my heart." I didn't know that was going to be the last. I would ask you back in a second if you were healthy and not sick. I would ask you back, but I know the Father has you. He knows when it's our time to go. I cherish all those memories. I hold on with the support of our family and friends. I hold on by a song. I pray Lord give me strength. I lose my faith and get it back. Most days, I cry and that helps with the healing. I still can't believe you are really gone. It seems like a whirlwind since that day six months ago. ***Please God, help me move along.***

SHATTERED HEART. My heart is broken in pieces. Shattered. How do I pick up and begin again? How do I live with you gone? How do I live with you gone? My heart beats differently now. It's so different with you gone. Why did you have to leave me? Why couldn't I go first? How do I live without you? I'm so lonely and sad. Will my heart ever feel again? Will it ever really heal with you gone? It's shattered. A shattered heart. Lord, I'm asking You to heal this broken, ever loving heart.

"My heart is troubled and restless. Days of suffering torment me."

JOB 30:27 NLT

WHAT IS YOUR STRUGGLE? What steals your peace? Does your fight seem long? Do you wake up and it's never really gone? What does your flesh wrestle with? Your heart knows best but how does it overcome when the battle is long and throws you into a funk? When each day seems the same and feels like a strain. Where does your help come from? Does it come from the world or the one who saved? Look to Him. Look to Him in a whole new way.

The heart is a beautiful thing. The heart beats so rapidly. The heart He gave. The heart is well until it's beaten down with grief and shame. Protect your heart from everything. Protect it like it's the only thing you hold. Protect it and when it gets broken, look to the Father that loves and knows.

It's almost been a year since I have seen your face. It's almost been a year and you feel further away. It's almost been a year, and each day, I wake up missing you, longing to hear you say, Dad I'm ready to go. I'm ready for this. Oh, how I long to hug you again. Oh, how I long to touch you and see you grow. Oh, how I long. How am I supposed to go on without you here? I don't understand. There are so many fears. How am I supposed to go on? Why did this happen to you? It's not fair. I just want to die with you. I want to be with you again. Help me, I'm crying out, help me to live again. Help me. Please help me move along and learn how to live with you gone. Please help me. I can't even seem to breathe. Help me see better days. Help me Father, help me stay.

JOY OVER DECEIT, I decree. I will live in joy and thanksgiving. Joy over deceit, I will choose. No evil shall enter in and rule.

"Deceit fills hearts that are plotting evil; joy fills hearts that are planning peace!"

PROVERBS 12:20 NLT

Do you focus on the good, the bad, or the ugly? Do you focus on yourself and think of things not worthy? Do you focus on religion, hate, and how it separates? Do you focus so hard you miss what He created? Where does your focus lie? Here with your eyes? Or the unseen the one way? Do you focus on Him coming back one day? Focus on the good. Focus on the truth. Focus on what He promised me and you. Watch, oh watch, how this focus changes you.

LOVE IS THE KEY. The key that never leaves you empty. He is love. He is the key to life. Love makes it alright. He is the key to happiness. Love gives hope. His love is enough. It conquers all sin. Love fights and love wins. Love is the greatest, heaven sent. My heart shall yearn to love well until the very end.

"The Lord loves those whose hearts are holy, and he is the friend of those whose ways are pure."

PROVERBS 22:11 TPT

I see love in people. Some I feel, most I see. The ones I feel never leave me empty. They always fill me up and pour out. They always stay until the final round. This love is a treasure and a gift. This love is something different, it's true, as I know this love truly comes from You. I know they love You, God, first, and they pour out from that deep love they have felt from our Fathers running well.

Is your heart depressed, sad, or maybe full of misery and gloom? Maybe it's hollow and you can't see through your fog. It's a real thing. Depression is so real. You don't have to stay there. It comes on so strong. You feel in a funk and despair. Wondering does anyone care? Do they understand what I am going through? Depression feels so hopeless and helpless. Pray to our God to come. To come and sit. To come and speak. To come and pull you through. He will be there no matter what, it's true. Cry out for help. You were never meant to carry this alone. Go to Him. He is waiting. Our Prince of peace. He sees.

"and the peace of God, which surpasses all understanding,
will guard your hearts and minds through Christ Jesus."

PHILIPPIANS 4:7 NKJV

Wave, after wave, after wave of truth. Wave, after wave, after wave with You. Wave, after wave, after wave You have come. Wave, after wave, after wave I can say, I am humbled and safe. In Your arms I shall stay.

WHAT MOVES YOU? What makes you lie still? What keeps you going when you have nothing left to give? What moves you? What makes you lie still? When the world is against you, and you gave your last I will. What moves you? What makes you lie still? Choose to be moved by the only one that gives the power to heal.

ARE YOU ROOTED AND GROUNDED IN LOVE? Are you rooted in love? Are you love? Do you share love? Do you receive love? Love is such a mighty thing. Love conquers hard things. *Love always wins at any cost.* Love was paid and bought. Love was the cross that day. Love, oh, Your love never fades. Help us share this precious love You have, as I know, when we love, people can change, and have.

Lord, all my days You have granted me Your grace. All my days You have given me Your peace. All You ask is that I receive. All my days You have never changed. All my days You have been showing me the way. All my days I never will miss. All my days are sealed with heaven's kiss.

A MOTHER AND HER CHILD. To raise them up and bring them forth knowing Jesus. To follow Him with every step they take. To talk to them about the hard things. To show them love in truth. To show them to always honor and glorify You. Being a mother, a precious gift given, to cherish her beautiful ones given by the God of heaven above. A mother that bears and cares what they may go through. A mother to always say, I love you. A source to come to. A mother to protect their heart, mind, and spirit with prayer, love, and truth. Oh, how being a mother is the greatest thing, it's true.

"Be kindly affectionate to one another with brotherly love,
in honor giving preference to one another."

ROMANS 12:10 NKJV

Being kind, generous, showing love and affection. Being kind no matter what. Kindness is considering others before themselves. Kindness grows and unfolds as the seed is thrown. Kindness is a gentle heart and friendly soul. Kindness is warm in nature and a hand to hold. Kindness always cares, never lets go, and never grows cold. Kindness is something we all long for.

Search me God and know my heart. Test me and my anxious thoughts. Show me right from wrong and where I truly belong. Search me God, oh search my heart.

WHAT ARE HOLDING ON TO? What are you yearning for? What does your heart beat for? Do you even know? What gives you joy like none before? Where's your source of security, money, and all things? Where does your heart go when it's looking for a way? Where does your heart go? Is it Him? Do you seek Him, the King of kings? Cry out, and seek Him over everything today.

"If they stumble badly, they will still survive, for the Lord lifts them up with his hands."

PSALMS 37:24 TPT

Are you dealing with insecurity in your heart? Doubt? Are you unsteady? Do you wonder if you are ever going to make it through? Cast your cares and find your hope in Him. It's true, He will be there when we fall. He will lift us up and help us stand tall. He will. He will. He will. Oh, He will. You will survive! You will. Look to Him. Look to Him, find hope in Him. Amen

Cleanse my heart. Renew my spirit. Cleanse my heart of those things that do not pertain. Cleanse them now. Renew my spirit that dwells in You now. Cleanse my heart. I want to be pure. Cleanse my heart and renew my spirit, as this is the only way I will truly flow.

THE HEART OF FRIENDSHIP. It's rare to find a friend that loves no matter what. A friend that hurts when you hurt. A friend that prays for you and your children. One that texts and says, hey, just wanted to see how you are doing and inputs the most amazing encouraging words at just the right time, all while receiving these, knowing full well she has the Holy Spirit dwelling inside of her, feeding me just what I need as I walk through my deepest valleys. This friendship is rare, and I pray she never leaves, but is always right there cheering me on, hearing my cries, battling those thoughts and lies. Thank you, Lord, as I know this is a true gift. Never let me forget.

"You are always and dearly loved by God! So, robe yourself with virtues of God, since you have been divinely chosen to be holy. Be merciful as you endeavor to understand others, and be compassionate, showing kindness toward all. Be gentle and humble, unoffendable in your patience with others."

COLOSSIANS 3:12 TPT

BE UNOFFENDABLE YOU SAY. How, when they come to slay? How, when they come to take? How, when the spirit inside them hates yours? How do I remain unoffendable? How? How do I? How do I remain humble and gentle? How? I don't know how. How do I begin to understand the torment of years I went through? How do I show mercy? How do I show kindness? How am I to be compassionate to the one that has always come and torn? I don't know how other than to live in full surrender of Your ways, Your truth, Your will. That's how I will choose.

We have this hope deep in our soul. We have this hope we shall call heaven our home. We have this hope, never shall we lose, if we always find our hope in You.

EMPATHY. UNDERSTANDING. COMPASSION. Maybe it's easier to give to someone hurting. Do you do the same when you're hurting? Do you give yourself time to feel? Do you give yourself time to go through? Do you have compassion and understanding when you are on the losing end and feel the lowest of lows? Are you gentle, caring and saying all the right things? How, oh how, do we help ourselves? How do we have empathy if the person is you? Help us, Lord. Help us see we should love ourselves too.

"Tolerate the weaknesses of those in the family of faith,
forgiving one another in the same way you have been
graciously forgiven by Jesus Christ. If you find fault with
someone, release this same gift of forgiveness to them."

COLOSSIANS 3:13 TPT

TRAUMA. A blow, agony in full course. The wound that isn't healing. The shock and suffering. The deep hurt and distress your whole being felt. Trauma. Shock. Trauma. Unforgiveness of what that person did to you for so long. Unforgiveness. Unforgiveness is really a thief. It's hard to believe. Help me forgive as You forgive me. It's one of the hardest things, I believe.

The gift of salvation, oh the price that was paid that day. The gift of salvation for all who call on His name. The gift of salvation, now that's something no man could ever take. The gift of salvation, oh how we live in His grace.

The heart of a father is to love, be gentle and never too harsh. To be the one to guide, provide, and love at all times. The father is so important. The safe place to run. He is the strength when in need of peace and security. He is, oh he is. A child that can depend on their earthly father is far more valuable than most things.

"Please listen and answer me, for I am overwhelmed by my troubles."

PSALMS 55:2 NLT

Please hear me when I am nervous. Please hear me when I am worried. Please see me and answer me when I feel uneasy. Please calm me when I feel tense. Please help me when I am overwhelmed and feeling agitated. Please help me. Do not leave me in this state of anxiousness and fear. Please Lord, I know You care. Please Lord, help me out of this despair. Help me. Please help me.

DO YOU EVER SEE SOMETHING THAT MAKES YOU CRY? That tears you apart? That just tugs a little more on your heart? When I see people struggle, hurting, or seem lonely, lost, scared, and confused, it just hits me. It makes me sad. It makes me want to grab them, hug them, and tell them they are loved and not alone. Why can't we be more vocal, more kind, more out of the box, look and not care? What if not caring what others thought or if they would accept these affirmations from you didn't hold you back? Could you just imagine what could be had? Could you just imagine if no one knew a stranger and we lived and loved like brothers and sisters? Could you just imagine the difference this would make? I imagine I would see more grace, more faith, more smiles, more people touched. Oh, start with me, Lord. Help me step out today with Your eyes of faith.

STRENGTH. I'm asking for Your strength. I'm failing and falling into a pit of despair. I need You now. I need Your strength to pull me through, to see me through this. I need Your strength more than anything. I need Your strength. Thank You, Lord for Your strength. I will walk through with You. I will not stop. I will walk through with You. I will walk all the way through with You. My eyes are on You, Lord.

CONFESS AND BELIEVE. Confess and believe. Confess and believe. You shall be saved. The greatest grace. The greatest gift we shall ever receive. Confess and believe.

"because if you acknowledge and confess with your mouth that Jesus is Lord [recognizing His power, authority, and majesty as God], and believe in your heart that God raised Him from the dead, you will be saved."

ROMANS 10:9 AMP

Our heart beats. It beats, beats, and beats again. Our heart beats until the very end. What is your heart beating for? Is it for love or for war? Check your heart and allow it to beat again. Allow it to beat well in your Fathers plan.

Does your heart stop when you get that phone call you never expected? What about getting that test result that says you have months to live? Does it stop when you see that child on drugs that stays addicted? Does your heart ever just stop to say, Lord, oh Lord, I'm asking You to see me through another day? Does your heart ever stop? I'm telling you today, when it stops, look up and pray.

"But be on guard, so that your hearts are not weighed down and depressed with the giddiness of debauchery and the nausea of self☒indulgence and the worldly worries of life, and then that day [when the Messiah returns] will not come on you suddenly like a trap."

LUKE 21:34 AMP

DO NOT BE TROUBLED. Do not let your heart grow cold to the ways of this world. Do not be tossed out by the winds and seas. Do not grow cold and turn in shame for your peace. Do not be selfish in this life as that will always turn around to bite. Do not grow cold in the heart, I pray. You do not know your last days. Be warm and loving in your heart. When the Messiah comes back you won't be caught in that trap, but smiling saying, I've waited for You to come and stay.

TAKE THIS UGLY OUT. Take this ugly out. My heart was beaten and bruised for so long I don't know what to do now that it's finished and done. The storm has passed, and it lasted so long. How do I get to a place I am good again? Help me get there fast. I can't live behind these fake smiles and masks any longer. Help me let go, help me today. I'm ready to seek Your face, Your way. Please help me let go today.

Is your heart ever so full you think it may burst? Does it beat so fast you think it's jumping off course? This heart is an amazing thing! It never lets you down and gives you air to breathe. This heart is an amazing thing. This heart was God's way of saying, you will always be ok, feel Me with your everything.

"And do not give the devil an opportunity [to lead you into
sin by holding a grudge, or nurturing anger, or harboring
resentment, or cultivating bitterness]."

EPHESIANS 4:27 AMP

Why is it so easy to hold on to resentment and a past grudge? The past that wreaked havoc on your life for many years! Was I mad because, in came strife with my marriage? Was I mad because I had to let my kids go and be held by my worst enemy? Yes. I believe yes. I also believe this is a key, an open door for the devil to wreck our world. He enters in, and multiplies this sin. He enters in, and leads you into a dark pit. He enters in, but he is not the one in control. He enters in, but only for a time, then he has to go.

I'm not ok. I'm not ok. I keep going deeper and deeper into my pain. I'm not ok. I can't let go. I try but there's a hold I can't explain. I can't let go. I need Your help. I need You now. I try to let go but fail again, and again. Just when I think I'm through it, something else comes in and reminds me again. Help me let go. My heart wants to love again and escape from all this bitterness.

If you had to choose to have your heart broken to love again, would you? Why is it so hard to forgive, mend, or heal a broken heart? Why does the heart feel so much pain? Father, You tell us this is all for our gain. Help our hearts Father, please help them today.

What your eyes see, your heart will feel. Your heart mends with a sound of praise. It mends when you hear a good report of grace. Your eyes may see good and bad, but focus on the good and your heart will be glad. Full of joy, full of strength, our heart is filled with You, everlasting glory.

"Eyes that focus on what is beautiful bring joy to the heart, and hearing a good report refreshes and strengthens the inner being."

PROVERBS 15:30 TPT

I need time. I need more time to let go. My heart isn't ready to hold and try again. It's not ready to be picked back up only to be disappointed in the end. My heart isn't ready, although I know it should be, but how many times can I put it out there and be left in defeat? How many times before you really change? How long before you really stop playing those games? How long, I need to know before I give back my heart and soul?

We give our hearts away. We give them away. We give our hearts away. We give them away. Yes, we give our hearts away. Jesus, for You, we give them away. Take them, have them, and grow them today.

"I don't depend on my own strength to accomplish this;
however, I do have one compelling focus; I forget all of the
past as I fasten my heart to the future instead."

PHILIPPIANS 3:13 TPT

Forget the past and all the burdens there. Forget the past and all its shame, you now have a new name. Forget the past, the torment, and lies. Forget the way you lived before you called on the name of the Lord. Forget it now and focus on the future and all His plans. Fasten your hearts and surrender to His ways, and let Him lead you into better days.

Help me, Lord. Help me, Lord. Help me. Please help me let go of it all. Help me release the deep of the deep hurt, pain, and agony. Help me, I can't seem to release the bitterness I have felt for so long. Help me release the bitterness, Lord. Help me release the bitterness I have left in me. Help me. Help me. Help me. Please Lord help me.

What causes such deep hurt pain? Is it the person or situation entertained? Is it something you are carrying? What makes you hurt? What causes that pain? I know one thing, I have a God that saves and loves at all times. I heard Him say, do not try to understand it all and trust Me in the hard times and the falls. I find myself trying to figure it out. I want to know the why, when, and how. Sometimes, that just isn't what He wants for us. He just wants our trust.

Find your hope in the only One. The only One that will never do you wrong. The only One that died to see you live. The only One that chooses to always forgive. The only One that can truly comfort you. The only One, it's Him we shall choose.

"And all who focus their hope on him will always be purifying themselves, just as Jesus is pure."

1 JOHN 3:3 TPT

The battered and bruised heart learns to love. That's a start. The battered and bruised heart. The cuts, tears, and torn apart. The battered and bruised heart learns to love, not by self, but how God does. When the battered and bruised heart forgets no more, it shows compassion from the depths of it all. When the battered and bruised heart releases its biggest enemy, it feels set free, and that's the place we shall yearn to be.

When your heart hurts too deep. When all you can do is weep. When one more day feels like a week. When you open your eyes to see. When your heart is so weak and feels like giving up. Where do you run to? Stop. Look up and breathe. He holds our hearts; He holds our peace. All He's asking is for us to surrender to Thee.

Understand little and trust much. Understand. Comprehend. Figure out little. Trust. Rely. Believe much. Don't worry your head. Don't worry your heart. Your health is more than those darts. Your health is more than those darts. Don't worry your head. Don't worry you heart. Don't go along just to fall apart. Don't worry your head, don't worry your heart. Trust me with everything, that's your start.

"So, we don't look at the troubles we can see now; rather,
we fix our gaze on things that cannot be seen. For the
things we see now will soon be gone, but the things we
cannot see will last forever."

2 CORINTHIANS 4:18 NLT

When the heart grows weary and takes another step. When your heart is humble and chooses no regret. When your heart forgives the worst of them. When your heart repents when you see no difference. When your heart stays true to what He has called you to do. When your heart says yes, when you don't see His plans that are set. When you pick your heart up and try again. When you know this world will soon be gone, you can live like eternity is your home.

What's your heart? What's your focus on? Is it the good, bad, or where they did you wrong? What's your heart in your deepest pain? Is it humble or full of rage? What's your heart when you never felt this much pain? What's your heart? Is it love at all odds Where's your heart, your focus, where is it at? Ask your Father to help it beat to His commands.

The heart knows betrayal and all evil things. The heart knows the barest way. The heart knows and feels the despair, and feels the weight, and the I don't cares. The heart knows love from above. The heart knows how to pour from His cup. The heart knows how to heal and forgive. Heart, do you know how to live again? Help this weary heart live again.

"Greater love has no one than this, than to lay down one's
life for his friends."

JOHN 15:13 NKJV

I can't fathom this love. The sacrifice, the boldness, the heart of
this love. Thank you, Lord, for this kind of love. It surpasses the
hard things, the unknown things, and the deep things. Thank you
for this love that bears all.

The heart doesn't lie, it feels. The heart doesn't lie, it aches. The heart doesn't lie, it breaks. The heart withstands the hardest things, and when it heals, it comes back with greater faith. With greater love. The heart doesn't lie, it takes grace. It takes grace to continue living this way. The heart is a special way of showing Jesus in ordinary ways.

The matters of the heart run fierce and deep. The matters of the heart should not flow to be empty. Pour those matters out. Don't let them lay stagnant in a heart that is full of doubt. Pour those matters out. Live free and with love, in a heart that is cleansed, and beating from above.

"Jesus answered him, " 'Love the Lord your God with every passion of your heart, with all the energy of your being, and with every thought that is within you.'"

MATTHEW 22:37 TPT

Lord, I am made from flesh. Help me die to it. Help me live with a passion, purpose, and plan. Help me to live, to love You, with all that I am.

Jesus came to do His Fathers will. Jesus came, so I could be filled. Jesus came, and He conquered it all. Jesus came, so I wouldn't fall. Jesus came, and I remember to say, Jesus came on all my hardest days. Oh, how Jesus always came.

Something tells my heart to stop. To stop loving and being kind. To stop going the extra mile as no one ever really cares. To stop loving at all cost and showing You everywhere. Something tells my heart, but I have power over it all. Something tells my heart You are the one in charge. Something tells my heart to love and beat again. Something tells me, and I know I will win.

Where does your heart truly lie in your fast? Are you doing it for pity or for love behind the mask? Where does your heart lie in your fast? Are you doing it to be seen and worthy? Are you doing it as a sacrifice to please? Where does your heart lie during your fast? Find where it lies and be in peace at last.

" 'We have fasted before you!' they say. 'Why aren't you impressed? We have been very hard on ourselves, and you don't even notice it!' "I will tell you why!" I respond. "It's because you are fasting to please yourselves. Even while you fast, you keep oppressing your workers."

ISAIAH 58:3 NLT

Your faith comes in like a flood on my day. It came in and I no longer choose to be phased. Your faith came in and the lights shine so clear. Your faith came in and showed my path is near. Near, oh near, is it all. Near, oh near, never shall I fall. Near, oh near, that day I lost all fear. Near, oh near, You took me to a place I have never been and called me to stay here.

A deep sigh of relief. I felt Your presence come in like a wave. It casted out the doubt and caused me to sing. To sing Your praise all my days. To sing my praise and never lose faith. Oh, the wave came upon, and still to this day, I have never felt the peace as I did on that day.

"Create in me a clean heart, O God, And renew a steadfast spirit within me."

PSALMS 51:10 NKJV

My core. Some moments I just feel You deep in my core. I feel like I'm strong and can withstand a war. Those moments I feel with my core, those moments could last a lifetime and I would never be torn. I know You have called us to go through the deep. You have called us to believe. I will once again see another day. This core You have made strong so I can withstand what trouble I may face.

The heart gets hurt and takes time to heal. This heart has shed more ways than I thought I could feel. This heart beaten, battered, bruised, and healed. This heart will love again like it's never been dealt with those feels.

"Don't be impressed with your own wisdom. Instead, fear
the Lord and turn away from evil."

PROVERBS 3:7 NLT

WHAT ARE YOU IMPRESSED BY? Looks, talents, money, and fame?
Are you impressed by Jesus or the world's claims? What are you
impressed by that fills your days? Choose to not be impressed by
mortal man ways, but choose to today to be impressed upon by the
only One that saves on your final day. He calls your name.

RESCUE US SINNERS. Rescue the lost. Rescue us, Lord, from it all. Rescue us sinners. Rescue the lost. Come rescue us now, this was all paid and bought. Rescue us, Lord, from the lies that hold us down. Rescue us, Lord, from the accusations that come around. Rescue us, Lord, we can no longer fight in peace. Rescue us, Lord, so we can be what You have called us to be.

MY HEART CRIES OUT! My heart cries out a little louder. My heart cries out. Do you hear me, Lord? Here I am, Lord. Do you hear me? My heart is crying out so loudly. Do you hear me, Lord? I'm crying out with a deep longing to hear from You. Do you hear me? Come rescue me like You always do. I'm crying out Lord. Save me. It's the only thing my heart knows to do. I'm crying out Lord, please come again like You always do.

"So above all, guard the affections of your heart, for they affect all that you are. Pay attention to the welfare of your innermost being, for from there flows the wellspring of life."

PROVERBS 4:23 TPT

The rock, the truth I stand on, is You. How could I faulter or be led astray? How could I not live by Your amazing grace? How could I walk ten days and never bow in Your name? How, oh how? I have learned a new way. A new way of a daily surrender and trust. A new way to only pour from your ever-loving cup. A new way is mine, being laid to death. A new way is you being my number 1.

SECURITY. In this world of unknown. Stock markets, gas prices, and all the rest. Lord help us live by faith and trust. Help us to live knowing You are the one. The one that supplies all our needs. Lord, You give us everything. When we go thinking we are in control, and life comes to a bust, please come lift us up. Show us truth. Give us peace to continue to honor You. We honor You by believing You are truth. We honor You by trusting You hold the keys. You hold our lives, and everything.

"But a time is coming and is already here when the true worshipers will worship the Father in spirit [from the heart, the inner self] and in truth: for the Father seeks such people to be His worshipers."

JOHN 4:23 AMP

I want to worship You, Father, in the spirit. I want Your heart to beat in mine. I want to show Your love and be kind. I want Your heart. I'm asking for Your heart to guide and lead me to You. I want Your heart to shine through.

Acknowledgments

Thank you to my very special family and friends for sharing their hearts and helping me with this precious book.

Lisa Machelett, your raw, honest heart will help so many. I appreciate you.

Julie Biles, you are the most kind, encouraging friend. I cherish you.

Laura, my sweet friend and Addy Declue. You are both so beautiful and your faith and trust in God blesses me so.

Tracy Null, you are so amazing and are always there the second I need you.

My sister Lindsey, your heart is the biggest and most soft and this is a journey I wouldn't want to take without you by my side.

My momma Brenda, your heart soars, loves every second, and keeps my heart in check every day.

Rita Krone, your heart has been broken in more ways than mine would ever want to know.

I love you all so.

LACEY WHITTAKER is the Founder of True Love Ministries. She yearns to flow only from the heart of Jesus. She lives in Bourbon, MO with her husband Justin and two daughters Addie and Liv. Her heart is for everyone to know that the most important relationship you can have is the one on one with our Father.